Dialogue for the Left and Right Hand

Dialogue for the Left and Right Hand

Poems by
Steven Cramer

Lumen Editions
a division of Brookline Books

ISBN 1-57129-033-8

Library of Congress Cataloging-In-Publication Data
Cramer, Steven, 1953–
        Dialogue for the left and right hand : poems / by Steven Cramer.
            72 p.   cm.
        ISBN 1-57129-033-8 (pbk.)
        I. Title.
PS3553.R2676D5   1997
811'.54--dc21   97-247
                                                                                    CIP

Printed in Canada by Best Book Manufacturing, Louiseville, Quebec.

10 9 8 7 6 5 4 3 2 1

Published by
Lumen Editions
Brookline Books
P.O. Box 1047
Cambridge, Massachusetts 02238-1047

For Hilary and Charlotte,
in memory of Marion O. Cramer (1917-1993)

Acknowledgments

My thanks to the editors of the following periodicals, in which some of these poems, or earlier versions of them, originally appeared:

AGNI: Section 3 of "Dialogue for the Left and Right Hand"

Alaska Quarterly Review: "Falling Asleep Over a Book About Consciousness"

The Atlantic Monthly: "The Night We Knew For Sure," "Villanelle After a Burial"

Boston Review: "The Glen"

Colorado Review: "The Ghost in the Wedding Photograph"

Crab Orchard Review: "Intensive Care," "The Obscure"

Greensboro Review: "When the Snow Thundered"

Harvard Review: "Filename"

Indiana Review: "Landlocked," "On Fire"

New England Review: "The Cloud Chamber"

Paris Review: "The Anniversary"

Ploughshares: "A Brief History of the Enclosure Movement"

Poetry: "The Work"

Triquarterly: "God's at the Top of the Stairs," "Hundreds of Paired and Spinning Seeds," "The Long Haul"

Some of the details in "Especially the Hair" are adapted from Timothy W. Ryback's article, "Evidence of Evil," which appeared in *The New Yorker*, November 15, 1993.

For their advice and encouragement, I am grateful to Gail Mazur, Robert Pinsky, David Rivard, Ira Sadoff, and Thomas Swiss. I am especially indebted to Hilary Rao for her invaluable suggestions regarding the order of the poems in this book.

Contents

Call the world if you please "The vale of soul-making."
Then you will find out the use of the world.

—JOHN KEATS

Dialogue for the Left and Right Hand

The Ghost in the Wedding Photograph

Wherever there's an emptiness to fill,
Look for me: devoid, concave, or hollow
Like a flute. If you find me, I'll sigh
Not out of melancholy, not from desire,
But as a kettle's whorl of vapor sighs,
An axle whines, an oar groans across a lake.
Losing me, you'll lose your sense of touch.

Although you can't conceive my face
Or remember much about my birth,
I'm not just a surface to disturb.
In the cool ache as your wrist refracts;
In a scumble of unreadable notes; in a name
That abrades when you say it, too often

You misspeak me and turn shy,
A child who runs to a parent and hugs
A stranger's knees. Once placid, I'm active.
Once a paper cup, once a trickle of water,
Now I'm thirst. But first I'm yearning,
Then yearning's aftermath: you never see
The Amaryllis lean toward the light.

Remember, when you're tempted to explain,
How contentment has made you rational—
Yes, you: lined up with your relatives,
Squinting from the shade of an American Elm.
I'm the one behind you, at the river's edge,
Who looks like you, who waves from the far bank.

Dialogue for the Left and Right Hand

1

Maybe all you want is to be punished.
Maybe that's why, over forty this fall,

You've taped to a mirror this snapshot
Of yourself at twelve: the wet threads

Of his bangs dangle into his eyes;
Pajama tops sport diamonds and fish;

His chin nests lightly into his fist
And his glare says *don't touch*.

For years you thought you wanted just
To scold him out of you, not to grieve

But to shush him till he's quiet.
Truth is, you can hardly remember

Afternoons he stole gum from *Kings*,
Nights he siphoned off his father's scotch.

Truth is, he's no child of yours. Why
Flinch at his merest footfall? Why ask *him*

To lift this middle-aged ache that sits
On your ribs like the knees of a neighborhood

Bully? Maybe you just want to be astonished
Then astonished. When you kiss your wife,

Whose mouth presses against her mouth,
Whose restlessness breathes into her hair?

And that night you leaned in a doorframe
And crumbled as she gripped your wrists,

Was the dryness in your throat his thirst?
Ask me to take your elbow, a voice says,

Teasing you one step closer. *Ask me
For a little help. You're almost walking.*

2 (Manasquan, 1960)

You can say this much about him:
With the muddy sand sucking at his feet
And sea wind drilling in his ears,
It's a wonder he's made it
This far onto the breakwater—

A birdless expanse of amber,
The sun rising, the horizon aligned
Across the August Atlantic, and you
A voice behind him that explains
The light makes a path on the water.

But he sees his mother and father
Striding from shoreline to horizon,
And a boy running after them,
Until he's swept out, over his head,
Just where the sky and water meet.

So you follow him and peer into
The green that shades to deeper green.
Gray seals eye him from the swells.
But something's beyond what he sees,
Farther out, after the horizon,

Something dangerous. *Show me,*
You say. But when you try to look
The sky dips down to touch the water,
A blue door like the door to a garage,
Because you can't see what he sees.

3

Child with us now was with us then—
With M. when his mother danced
Handstands without underpants,

So now he cringes, as from a punch,
If anyone says *cunt;* with R. when her aunt
Yanked her hair into a stinging bun

And made her wear it that way every day;
With C. when his father crawled toward him,
Balls dangling through his boxer shorts

. . . *Like pink bells,* he murmurs to himself,
Till everyone in the room is murmuring,
Headfuls of muttering grownups,

The room silent, wishing it hadn't heard,
Wishing it could take back what was said.
The room's a clearing in a forest, circled

And circled and missed. A pine forest,
Resin-scent lifting from the floor of needles,
A face under every tree. The child on our left

Is whispering: *don't let them see you cry.*
So R.'s tongue pushes out her bottom lip;
M. purses his, as if moistening a reed;

And C.'s mouth twists and seems to fill
With rotten meat. Meat of grief
Around the table where blame got passed

From plate to plate. We cross our legs,
Uncross our legs; tuck them underneath us.
A sister's face, a brother's face, the face

Of Mother looking at Dad's face, Dad's face
Glaring through the steam off his plate—
The child says *to be looked at is to die.*

And so we die, and return to the ghosts
Who wept and laughed down our hallways.
With the child's ears we hear the keys

Pecking, adulterous, at the front lock;
The child's nose sniffs alcohol, tobacco,
Sweat and talc drifting up the stairs

After all the ghosts have gone to bed;
With the child's nerves we feel the cold
Spot inside memory. Each touch proves

The ghosts are real. *Can't you see*
The ghosts are real? the child insists.
For a moment we don't see, then we see.

4

Now you must be wondering what it feels like.

Can you sense the heaviness begin to lift
Like a spring tide rising to your attic window?
Do you recognize a new pulpiness to words—
Sweetgum, sourwood, bitternut—
Because to name them is to taste them?

Remember how you worked to earn defeat?

A fresh way begins by disowning loyalty.
Pay it back into the palm that made yours sweat.
Now picture a den,
An oak-paneled den,
An empty, oak-paneled den.

Place in it whoever wouldn't let you speak.

Now speak and permit no backtalk.
Walk out and don't look over your shoulder.
Even if you *prefer* the smoky light in there;
Even if you grew up breathing its paternal scent;
Even if, as you grasp the lion's-head knob on the door,

A voice says *I love you,* and means it.

5

When you go you don't take the pain with you.
You can't kill it with a swipe of disinfectant.
When you're not home, home is empty,
The porchlight burns for you.

It's not too late; I'd talk with you openly.
I'd wash my neck in the word "downpour"
Before you thin out to a minute hand,
And the bone in my throat loosens.

But oh, *your* voice: it's the sound
A rusty pump handle makes if I'm thirsty,
Or a wooden rhythm instrument with ribs
That croaks when raked with a stick.

Your speaking as I speak once scared me,
The way we fear our faces in night windows.
Grief attuned to richness of spirit, now
We know how much it matters if we lie.

Falling Asleep Over a Book
About Consciousness

Before we could hear ourselves think
And learned to heed the brain's
Furrowed code for worry,
Introspection, says this book,
Boiled down to hunger
And the wisdom not to eat
Our own bodies. Waking me
From my nap, the cat
Nested between my knees
Pumps at my thigh with her forepaws,
A throwback to her newborn
Thirst, I think—instinctive
As that afternoon I watched geese
Lift off Concord Reservoir, and stopped
Overhearing myself long enough
To pass an ant from hand to hand
Twice. I loved watching it
Freeze between each knucklebone
And try to dig in. Eons of evolution
For that moment of focus.
But often it's the mind's *un*rest
In all its pandemonium of hurts
And wants that hankers for attention—
Its nostalgia for the dead, its lust
At a touch, and its aches
That numb like the tug of waves
Burying the body feet-first . . .
And if these, then by association,
Its self-love welling in my eyes
Every time Truffaut's *400 Blows*

Ends with its frieze of adolescence,
Antoine's grainy look staring back
From the shore, the ocean behind him
Orphaned between tideline and sky.
Of course, it's his human abandonment
That turns so completely toward us.
And who isn't just as likely to cry
Thousands of frames earlier
At the feral way he gulps a pint of milk?

In the Blue Room:

A doorknob turns on the closet door.
A boy wakes to the *chick* of the latch
And opens his eyes, and in the blue light
From the window sees, or thinks he sees,
The door open an inch or two, no more.

The boy should leap from bed but can't.
Blue bureau, blue bedframe, blue chalkboard
Whose dust rubs off when touched,
White as the speechlessness in fear.
The boy should run down the hall but won't.

From the large bedroom across the hall,
A man's voice, a woman's voice, arguing.
Their voices paint streaks across his room
Like the red streamers inside jellyfish.
Every night he hears them he's afraid

The man's voice will sting the woman's,
Or the woman's voice will sting the man's.
So he dangles his feet over the bedside
And makes the bed a raft, the voices
Sloshing on his lap and swirling green.

It feels good sitting waist-deep in this water.
Jellyfish, he whispers, a see-through word,
A seaflower floating in the shallows. *Jellyfish*—
Until he's not afraid of anything, not even
The door he must have dreamed was opening.

The Anniversary

Not just because a child draws him—pie-faced and frontal,
Grinning—it's hard to watch the man's head and hands take shape
From a black magic marker, despite the other colors in the box:
The sparse hair on his forehead, the eye-orbits without pupils,
A hook, like an inverted question mark, to signify the nose,
And his mouth a lipless grimace, really a snarl.

Two X's represent what might have touched, waved, even spanked,
And the eyes' white squint might be the child's memory
Of the man's manic visitations: those babblings of happiness
Sweeping through the house, until everyone in his wake
Went a little crazy too, slugged dumb by his anecdotes about
     the war,
Words misfiring like the Spitfire he'd mimic, arms flung wide
     like wings.

But now the child sketches the woman: mouth upturned
(As he works on this he nibbles his lip, and squints, and frowns),
Her lips a rich scarlet—which, like her orange hair, seem to ignite
As he deepens the red to widen her smile, then adds wife-
     like loyalty
With brown pupils in the corners of her eyes, then darkens them,
So she lavishes regard on her husband who can't look back.

Again he reaches for black, blocks out a torso, neck and arms;
Stops. Compared to her, the husband's just a tracing.
But they're both dispiritingly flat. They'd be cold to the touch.
If you were the parents discovering this sketch—in his toy box
Or between the boxspring and mattress of his bed—you'd worry.
Now the marker scratches the spot where their hands meet,

But instead of a hand, he scrawls a tangle of lines,
A net that grows and seems to fix them there. And still
He's not finished, one hand hovering above the bright colors,
His face wrinkling, relaxing, until at last he chooses green—
For jealousy? for ghosts? for a feeling he can't name?—
And writes across the top: *The Anniversary*. Puts his marker
   in the box

Because he thinks he's done. Takes it out again. Adds a date.
   Looks up.

When the Snow Thundered

When the snow turned angry and thundered,
I told its bad mood, its white mood
At home under drifts, on collapsed
Ladders buried and iced over,
To go to hell—

I wanted to see what the squirrel sees,
Leaping from branch to branch,
All blameless precision. I shut my eyes
And snow chilled my eyelids.
Now I confess

The squirrel's a dropped glove, the snow's
A rumor, a rumor about me. How easy
In snow to face nothing!—
As if every direction
Faces the dead.

When my father told me to shovel snow,
I told him to go to hell.
He was a glove buried under a drift.
Now he's an ash tree, some flaking
Bones in my hand.

So I spread rumors about the snow
To check if he's listening:
Those cars are sliding toward funerals,
Their criss-crossed skid marks
Limbs of the ash

Branching on a hand never raised
Against him, the hand I held back,
Keeping my winter gloves on,
So he could never touch
My sweating palm.

But he's stopped listening. Yes,
I'm certain he's stopped listening.
When I heard the snow thunder rumbling
Like the chest of his winter clothes
I dragged to the attic,

That was a rumor too. Yes and no. I mean
His chest thundered so badly I rubbed
My hands on my knees; now I confess
His anger's just this stranger
Outside shoveling snow.

Regarding the Enemy

Of course it's dangerous
Waiting up for him—
Especially stripped down to my underpants
And sweating, my mouth sour,
As if he'd licked my tongue in my sleep.
I'm a boy crashing fighter airplanes into the sea,
Dead and not dead as usual. He's the crush
Of the driveway's gravel under his wheels
Before he comes stumbling in.
So of course I help him lug bricks
From one corner of the basement to another
Then lug them back. This is *work*.
This is what a man does to *contribute*.
Then he takes the bathroom mirror off its wall
And claims it's a photograph of me—
This is knowledge that will last me all my life.
Soon there are hundreds of me glistening
With his sweat
And only one of him.
I could choose not to believe a thing he says.
I could stop wishing to be anyone,
Anyone, but me. I could name myself myself.
The night I do will be the night
Women's hands soften my wrists like wax—
On my right, on my left, overhead,
Gorgeous women who know it's not cool
To be loud and hazardous and insistently ill.
Enough, these women hiss,
And on that night I'll listen
When they count to three, reach down my throat,
And grip my heart in their three hands
Till the hundreds of him become the one of me.

Filename:

As for credentials, I'm no one
I don't want to be right now.
I chew this cinnamon stick
& turn its loggy splinters over
On my tongue, knowing nothing
Can replace a Marlboro Light.
Yes, I still find the clarity
Of quiet quietly terrifying.
Yes, my imagination lisps
& frets as much as ever.
No, Coleridge would insist,
That's not the esemplastic glue
Of the imagination, but fancy
Simple & impure, unlike
The night vision visiting
A monk five centuries ago,
Who trudges up the staircase
At San Marco. On his cell wall,
Fra Angelico's Jesus,
Splendid & untouchable, rises
Over a field of cornflowers.
My imagination, though, concludes
He must hate miracles
& his friar's mind, *fuck the spirit*
That paints immortal frescoes.
As for the afterlife, only
When I'm desperate do I think
That's where my father rubs
His thumb & forefinger together,
Like someone testing silk, above
A lit match—alive & mad again
For one more cigarette. Before I die

I want just one indelible sentence
On my lips, what nobody can say
To me but me. So answer, father,
& I swear I'll never bother you again.

A Brief History of the
Enclosure Movement

"So you see," said Keats, "our English countryside
Was once communal grazing land, before
These fenced-in greens & amber greens
Of private farms." As we continued
Walking arm in arm from bourn to bourn,
He explained Soul-Making & what he really meant
By atoms of intelligence. Snow fell;

We crossed the Heath; he said belief
Came slow to him, like waking up
Came to me this morning, a little sick
But still pulling on my boots
For winter errands. It was then
That from a postcard on my wall,

Severn's charcoal of the living Keats
Looked away with the disinterest
He called thought. "When you get back,"
I heard him say, "write something
Without artifice, even without beauty,
Something simple, watchful, true."

Then I felt even sorrier for Severn,
Always the efficient, gallant one
In those two pitiable, foul-aired rooms,
His patient one day begging for the grave,
The next, his books; & below the corner window,
No snow twirled on the Spanish Steps—
All the city's fountains drained & cleaned.

To the One Who Is Good

Assume, at first, you can't expect
This light angling through apple trees
In an untended orchard. Sun and shadow
On the mountains. Stationary clouds.

Accept you're not the only spirit here
Trying to speak, as everybody else
Is singing underwater. Who forecast
A light so distilled? Not them, not you.

Audience doesn't matter, nor do nights
Of poets reading to their friends
About the golden syntax of their friends.
Audience means everything, to anyone

Willing to listen till the dead applaud.
What you'll make is what you'll make.
So accomplish it, stitch by restitch;
A knot slackened, the weave tightened

In that web. Everlasting labor, yes—
But also a future, enough room, histories.
No, honest art's not carpentry, and yet
The sturdiest houses have this lived-in look.

The Glen

A little riff I love slipped my mind
    This morning when I tried to whistle it.
        Because I couldn't rescue it,

I thought back to our argument, one word
    Misjudged like the slip of a peeler,
        Leaving us both to heal,

A tone of voice I chose to misconstrue.
    So you walked out. And I
        Listened to the gods

Turning down all my invitations,
    Until one beckoned with a green
        Echo from a drainpipe,

Just large enough to let me regress
    And scramble through to the glen:
        How predictably beautiful

The emerald glint off the leaves,
    And their smell of chlorophyll
        Like come scent from bedsheets;

How evocative the scrolls of birchbark,
    Leathery and speckled, a lizard's skin.
        Not *before* but *again,* I said,

As if to undress the raiments of memory,
    Undo the snaps, fumble underneath
        With the adolescent freshness

Of a boy who strips, circled by his friends,
　　And they applaud, awed and a bit
　　　　Taken back by the purple

Blush of his erection.　Before
　　Affection makes us bicker again,
　　　　Before the child we're considering

Takes on flesh, just when we're busiest
　　Sweeping out a corner of its afterlife,
　　　　Let's reassemble the glen,

Where the gods are brutal and guiltless;
　　Where memory's just a flash
　　　　Of dread at the salamander's

Lustrous skin; where the child I can't help
　　Being scuttles up the streambed,
　　　　Measuring his steps along slick stones,

Until only his thin whistling remains.

Hundreds of Paired
and Spinning Seeds

They had no name for the sick light
The day they found out, or the days after—

Green draining out of the neighbor's maple
From the top down, until it was all

Brown edges and stains. When they tried
Loving the fastidious watercolors

Their nieces taped to the refrigerator door,
Even the fat-faced clouds announced rage

In a cumulus burst, and even the sun,
With its nimbus of spikes, knew to curse.

Even the babyish symmetries hurt—
Rayflowers with pink petals and violet disks,

The sky sky-blue and the dirt dirt-brown,
Girl and dog a sexless pair of sticks.

And still they stared and stared,
Until she exhaled a grief

They called *After the Miscarriage,*
Or *Not the End of the World.* That was before

The maple flooded their neighbor's porch
With hundreds of paired and spinning seeds.

The Night We Knew for Sure

The night we knew for sure,
I sat with three or four men in a bar,
Men who need a drink before they'll speak,
Whose voices shrink to mutterings
If they touch the cusp of feeling.

Then in walked my dead father,
All compressed hilarity and need—
Stooped hands-in-pockets shuffle,
Unbuttoned lamb's wool cardigan,
Its country club insignia two putters
Crossed against the C above his heart.

I knew he'd sit across from me
Reluctantly, and not look up.
Then he'd stand and amble to the bar,
Flipping quarters into the till
To charm the waitresses.

I knew no one makes the old man see
What he doesn't want to see, especially
When he's drunk and full of feeling.
Then, from a room across the bar,
Where I knew you lay in labor,
I heard our firstborn cry.

The Long Haul

Then the morning arrived, and the idea
Of you surfaced, almond-shaped, on the ultrasound.
I looked but wasn't sure of what I saw,
Like the faithless who peer into their hands.
But you, gene braiding gene, helix
Of filaments, mote of multiplying cells,
This is your trimester of blindness,
After which your salmon-eyes narrow. In you
The ocean rises, establishing memory.
You're passive as eelgrass, sleek as a seal,
And *Mother*'s at best two watery syllables, a radio wave.
How I hope *Father* won't be that grittier sound,
The male bellow I shrank from,
As from the stink of live bait. Asleep,
I've kissed you. Asleep, I've stroked your hair.
I've heard the heartbeat where there is no heart,
A *wish wish wish* at two beats per second.
I've even troubled you into a troubled child,
Child eyeing the world through a straw
When the world's bad company—
Oh, leave it to grownups to press
Thumb dents into your fontanel,
To awaken shame, to scare up
Numbness, to follow you
The way the moon follows on long drives,
Unveiling more of its funhouse face each night.
Little nuance, don't perfect your courage yet,
Don't cope as talking dolls cope, button-eyed vacancies . . .
You are the self
Untouched by fibs about the self.
Dividing inside you, wrinkle of our flesh,
There's sadness and happiness enough for the long haul.

Especially the Hair

Who knows how many times a day
Evil squints at us, and then
Selects some other body
More hunched, paunchy, more rosy
Around the eyes, where weakness shows?
Or a body too young to put to use,
Like Charlotte's, which totters
Into my arms to be carried to the car.
The wind sweeps snow off roofs
In a stark white squall she smiles at.

But last night as she whimpered
In her sleep, I read about the hair:
Two tons stored twenty pounds per box,
Braids, curls, womanly tresses,
The children's hair peach-fuzzy,
Colorless—so brittle every crate
Released updrafts of mothy dust
Finer than this snow fluttering
Into Charlotte's bangs, brown
With reddish tints, and for her age

Stunningly thick. And it was safe
On this seasonably cold December night
To wonder what protected them,
Those expert curators of memory,
From the sheer unholiness of having
Had to itemize the brushes,
Mirrors, razors, forks, spoons,
Knives, but especially the hair—
Hair that still gives up a trace
Of cyanide, hair as evidence,

Hair as history, hair as just
A body part to bury with respect . . .
At which point I dozed, woke,
Flicked off the book light, slept,
As once or twice Charlotte yelped
And smiled, maybe, at the dark:
Same smile she'd have given the boys
Who hoisted her into a truck—
Another infant without posture, muscle
Tone, two teeth, but with enough

Hair to harvest, cure, and gather
Into bales with the rest; to market
To felt and textile factories
At twenty pfennigs per kilogram;
Good for thread, the soles of shoes,
Rope, cloth, carpets, mattress stuffing,
Lining stiffeners for uniforms, socks
For submarine crews, insulation
For the boots of railroad workers,
For delayed action bombs. Same smile.

Strange Fire

What's made God so touchy in *Leviticus?*
The boredom of rehashing verse after verse
Of His own instructions about burnt offerings?—
How to flay and disembowel a ram, a bullock,
A turtledove; how to wash the legs and innards;
How to cleave a pigeon's wings and pluck its feathers;
How to cook flour, then mingle it with oil . . .
All this to send sweet savour unto the Lord.

Whatever's gotten into Him, the Nameless One's
Inscrutable, as usual, in Chapter Ten
When His fire comes out from the altar,
Consuming the rumps of the bullock and the ram,
And their kidneys char, and the cauls
Of their livers shrivel, and the congregation
Falls on their faces, and Aaron's eldest sons
Decide to improvise a little on the ritual
And light their censers, sprinkling the flames
With incense, so that a second fire
Burns them to a crisp.

                What were they guilty of?
An extra dash for His blood-speckled tabernacle,
A pinch of myrrh to freshen the stink of burnt fat:
To the Almighty these amount to *strange fire,*
A gift too unscripted to be holy. Ever
The interpreter, Moses takes Aaron aside:
"The Lord has spoken, *I will be glorified.*"
And Aaron holds his peace.

Some say he's remembering that incident
With the golden calf, his single lapse.
I'm convinced he's pissed, but can't say so,
Like the child who waddles to his father
With a stuffed goat or a crayon
And gets cuffed, just because Our Lord
Of False Moves loves to hear us plead, *Why me?*

Which is what a friend cried when he learned
His test results, and sobbed into my neck.
All I did was hold on and say nothing,
Because the answer is there is no answer,
Though occasionally we still glance up
The way my neighbor did, whose daughter,
Lungs a phlegmy nest of cysts, played tag—
Sputtering at her brothers to *wait up!*

"Maybe she'll live to six," he said, and looked
Skyward, as though to add "God owes me one."
His tone was part misery, part rebellion—
Like Aaron's, who refuses to eat the goat
And lets the scorched carcass lie there,
A blackness he wouldn't have anyone digest,
Not even his surviving sons, and says to Moses—
Had I eaten the sin offering today, would it
Have been accepted in the sight of the Lord?

Ode to Joy

Forty-two years ago: twin sisters dead
By lightning in New Hampshire; subway fares
Hiked to fifteen cents; a downpour turned

To deluge, turned to drought; an air battle
Faked over Western Europe. As though tragedy
Thrived on trivia. Forty-two years later,

I'm staring at this *New York Herald Tribune*
From the morning of my birth, as star by star
Snow rises on my daughter's jungle-gym

And sparrows scatter husks of seed. The gap
Between their skittery hunger and my reading
Is a nameless black and white: the words I need

For how my hands trembled when I plucked
This news from a kitchen drawer of dull knives
The day we emptied out my parent's house.

Bag after bag of bedpans, cracked china,
Men in fedoras eyeing us from Polaroids,
Crates of shoe trees, jigsaw puzzles, two dead

T.V.'s: everything we chucked a fact
That qualified as truth. The truth is, though,
I'm distracted by a crow outside my window,

How it glides on sleek, unruffled wings,
And riles the birds hovering near the feeder
Who sink to peck black seed-chaff on the snow—

A lesson in appetite to show my daughter,
Nearly three, right now awake and crying,
Although these days just buttoning her shirt

Without a scene seems cause enough for joy.
A loss, for her, is waking to a room
That's parentless, then isn't; but for me,

It's when we watch her favorite video
About the boy who, having lost his father,
Learns how to appreciate Beethoven—

No, not the music, but the genius himself
Who rents the dead man's upstairs studio
And turns a room that's holy for the boy

Into an aerie strewn with parchment, stinking
Of ink and eggs. Cross-legged on the floor,
He pounds out fragments of his *Ode to Joy,*

Piano legs sawed off so he can feel
Vibrations through his ass and fix the score.
The boy wakes up to plaster in his eyes,

Convinced a madman's taken his father's place.
But by mid-video, he's jotting questions
In the Conversation Books, and my daughter,

Spinning as she wrestles off her shirt,
Is bored. When Maestro sends the boy for pens,
It's his clogs across Vienna's cobblestones

That pull her back, not a kid named Christoff
Sprinting to keep his father figure happy.
In the lakeside scene that really gets to me,

They flick thistle into the mirrorless water—
Fictional child and legendary fact
Loitering, not speaking, until Christoff

Scribbles his wish that no one ever died,
And Beethoven recalls the dawns his father
Yanked him out of bed to improvise.

Watching them, you'd think we might not need
A challenge all the time. Then Beethoven
Turns, and listens with an intimate flinch

To nothing Christoff hears—all the while
Birdsong and the *Pathétique* on the soundtrack.
What's music to one is silence to the other.

The Cloud Chamber

Can anything be said for us? Men
Unwrapping towels from our waists
To coil them, by instinct, into whips;
Some of us hunkering down, naked
On thin benches, elbows on thighs
As though to hide our average dicks;
Or squinting at our combination locks,
Some arguing girls or war, hitching up
Our shorts and taking affectionate
Punches to our muscle groups.
Mostly we talk about money.

                         I'll bet
A few still keep a twelve-year-old inside,
Designated sissy of the seventh grade
Who can't catch or throw, can't hit,
But who can take a sawed-off cider jar
And build a Wilson Cloud Chamber himself.
I'd love to rebuild mine from the bottom up,
From its pedestal of smoldering dry ice
To the sponge gasket soaked in alcohol,
The metal plate on top electrified
And nestled in a ring of vaseline.

It was a cell that rained inside,
The supersaturated atmosphere
Condensing on atomic particles,
Their trails white wakes as they shot out
From a thumbtack dipped in jeweler's paint.
I'd love to smash it too, with the simmering
Humiliations of seventh grade inside—
Especially the locker room where Eslinger

Inscribed my shirt with his autograph
Of piss. What did I expect from him?
Certainly not his butt-headed approval
For the headlock I fixed on the only boy
Weaker than me, leaping up and down
Like a schoolyard Bruno Sammartino.

So why this fresh urge to corner Eslinger
Who's probably a father now, cursing out
His son's wild pitches in their driveway?
Suppose I found him, and suppose after all
These years he said *I'm sorry,* got right down
On his knees and begged me for forgiveness—
What could I say back, as his boy's next throw
Veered off to disappear beneath a hedge?

Intensive Care

Decades since I hated like that—
A loathing, that is, so deeply brewed
I could sniff it wafting off the men
I stood among, my jaw stinging with nicks,
The trolley teetering on its trackbed, and me
Too scared to stray from the hydraulic doors
Convulsing open and shut at every stop.
Farther back, the less astringent traces
Of the jobless, who'd slept without sheets
And woke and didn't care, or cared
For all I knew—

A 17-year-old, slipping my wrist
Through the chrome loop overhead,
The Green Line dipping below Boston,
I'm going to work the thought I kept
At bay on Tremont Street, where Chinatown
Flanked the Combat Zone, and New England
Medical Center elbowed out the projects.
Head pressed against the 8 A.M. wind, of course
I was an abject sight, but why
Bitch about it now?

Because
I loved someone in Vermont, and it's time
The heart blurted into this chronicle?—
Fantasies of her belly and breasts and face
Stroking me home to Devotion Street
(The name too flagrant to invent),
Hair a greasy tangle, because they'd placed me
Right away on pots. Seven hours of scouring
Each aluminum cauldron to perfection;

No, that's a lie. Too weak
At first to lift them from the rinse,
I got good at loitering by the dumpster
For a pair of butt-to-tip cigarettes
Just before break at ten. Still,

I loved someone in Vermont, that much
Is true enough, even when her letters
Grew more informational each month.
Notice how the heart muscles in,
Even when I want to curse until
I make a strident music—say, my own
Insuck of breath as a sheeted cadaver
Slid from a lift reserved for freight;
Or when the boss promoted me
To the Pediatric Ward, the kids
Glisteningly sick or broken,
Each cigarette a mercy as I wheeled
My steamtruck to and from Intensive Care.

All I wanted was to hate. Now look at me:
Lifting my eyes toward the girl my age
Born with no spine, two nurses feeding her
Through the grid of her chrome scaffold.
Her boneless torso in its smock, her face
Sagging in flaps on the left side, her teeth
So grey I sickened when she grinned—
Even these, all earth by now, I recall
With whatever loving horror I can muster,
Memory itself like that dazzling contraption
That held her body more or less upright.

The Obscure

That was the winter I pegged, point-blank,
An iceball into Jeffrey Goodman's face.
Huddled behind the ramparts
Of our snowfort, we were teammates,

So even before I chucked
My planet of gravelly slush
I knew this was a first:
Gratuitous betrayal without skill.

The instant the projectile hit
With a satisfying crack and splatter,
And I saw Jeff's face convulse
Into a flush of red snot and tears,

I lapsed into bawling too,
But not on Jeff's behalf, unless
I wept for what I'd run smack into—
The urge to hurt at the heart of love

Granular and tough as the skin
Of that iceball. I know a fist
Of snow still hardens in my chest;
I know it when I find the one

Right word to spit at you,
Then say it again, and say it again.
All the while a twin voice pleads
What the fuck's with you? Let up Let up

And those two voices, wrangling,
Churn up a sludgy underturf of guilt
Dense as the topsoil Jeff and I
Scratched at every spring,

Unearthing birdskulls, ribs,
Coiled grubs, that dirt
A whiff from childhood I flinch from
Whenever I recall the slurs

That sent him blubbering home. Once
I thought you'd make whatever says them
Go away. Now some nights it wakes me,
A stray cat yowling as it mates or fights,

Or a mask I claw at, can almost taste,
As if I'd thrust my tongue into that ooze
I slapped across Jeff's face; and soon
I'm lapping at it, then whispering

Into its ear, a post-
Coital jerk who thinks he's gotten lucky,
Who hears it murmuring beside him as it sleeps,
Who breathes lightly so as not to wake it.

A Cool Dark Place

Ok, he's really mad now, pissed
Enough to burst out of his house
And stumble, ruddy and mumbling,
Toward the wire-haired professor
In a flannel robe, bending
From his porch to take *The Times*.
For a millisecond it's not clear
Who is scaring who. *Whom,*
The professor would insist,
His fury rarely surfacing
Except as a passion for grammar,
And patently no match for this
Irish teenager in a fit—
One hand raised as if to slice,
Karate-style, a Corolla's
Sideview mirror off its stem.
Neck thick as the prof's calf,
Yet with a face sweetly
Boyish in its beardlessness,
He pauses to tuck a stray
Feather of hair behind his ear.
The prof, granted this truce,
Retreats to witness the rest
From his hall, recalling
As he twists the deadbolt lock
How he once punched a mirror
And watched, enraptured,
As the map of the fracture
Imprinted on his fist filled
With his blood. Whose face
Does *he* yearn to smash
In his cool dark place

Where strangling his dad's
Commendable, where he laughs
To see his mother cowering?
In the *Metro* section of the news
The professor risked a beating for
This morning, enough anger
Should boil and spill over
To last an afternoon. Till then
He's reduced to prying
Into a neighbor's rage; and since
He respects the imagination,
He puts the boy back inside
His triple-decker, emptying
Buck-shot into the family
Magnavox, then retiring
To a basement mattress,
Over which a pegboard's thronged
With clippers, saws, trowels.
But now, as if he'd heard
This trespass on his inner life,
The kid quivers, straightens,
Swaggers downstreet to another car,
Then lets go with a kick
That leaves the mirror dangling
Like an eye popped from its socket.
And finally, backhandedly—a high
Sign in some ancient brotherhood—
He waves back up the street,
Just letting the professor know
Their furious collaboration's through.

To Consider Is to Observe the Stars

Just once I'd like to see myself
Through someone else's eyes, and thus
Get it in my head that what I'm up
Against, in being me, is not as awful
As those Kodacolor posters of Earth
Plunked down into the blue-
Black absence of atmosphere—
Olympian sight for the astronauts.
That's not a recognition scene I need.
And I'm against the constellation
Of shock and milder awe a child encounters
When he stumbles on his Uncle George,
The one war hero among his kin, discoursing
With a sweating mug of Ballantine. The sun
Through a block-glass window behind him
Hides his face. The kid's bright enough
To know he feels no sadness, but he can't
Help studying this silhouette whose daily ale
Lessens his stutter, and who could no more
Navigate this squall of sibilants
Than recite Oedipus's speech before
He blinds himself. George takes a swig,
For the first time aware he's not alone,
And the *sh- sh- sh-* that's building up
To *show me how you make a muscle, kid,*
Does more than dampen the kid's spirit.
It makes him disappear, until he grows up
Moderately articulate. Assuming he's not me,
I'd love to hear what he's thinking
On a particular winter night in Vermont
When he observes the stars he doesn't know
From planets, and considers how the gods we used

To recognize looked down on us—if not
Benignly, then at least with some belief
That every earthbound mortal knew his fate
Was his character, and stuck to it. Or just
As often didn't, and wound up falling
Into a drunken sleep and drowning
In the bile of his own unenlightenment,
Self-knowledge, even then, in short supply.

God's at the Top of the Stairs

It can't feel like homework.
If it requires penmanship,

Don't do it. If there's no red
Magic marker, no edible

Paste, no aroma of mimeo blue
To push a face into, forget it.

Who wants to sidle up close
To the moment inside the moment

Inside the moment, if it's not
An apple skin peppered with cloves?

Stop listening for the wind
Somewhere hushing the sweet William;

Don't demand enlightenment
From the bindweed between railroad ties

In Dover, New Hampshire—
Where once, on mushrooms, you swore

"The Brown's" brown mailbox
Shouted *brown* so loud

World married Word and moved in;
And stop waiting for your ship

While the dock rots. *God's*
At the top of the stairs. You'll see

If you sit on the edge of the bed
And stare at your feet and say

Here I am for damn good reason.

Some of His Answers

for my brother

Which summer was I old enough to wade
Past the breakers? When did I take up the guitar?
I hear you passing these questions back and forth.
Isn't it better to ask if I *was* that boy?

Here, I'm learning to walk by not walking.
Sometimes I lurch and lose my step, waist-deep in surf
So bright it blinds, stumbling on a substance like rockweed.
Here, nothing I touch touches back; what's beyond reach

I turn into—the way, when you're terribly thirsty,
Even your eyesight is dry. And still I can't tell you
How much or how little I see, the breezes here so cool
I'm relieved I don't have to feel again

That rash I'd get when angry, that tightening
In my chest when I scolded my children.
Even nostalgia, now, resembles a broken tool
Uncovered in the basement, its hinge

Rusted shut, no clue to what it was used for.
Forgive me if this confuses you. I only know
It's like finally understanding color, or reaching
The untouchable spot between your shoulder blades.

Soon I'll know more and won't speak at all, forgetting
How old I was when I first put my head underwater,
How skillfully my hand formed chords, and I'll walk
Easily into it, like the blind

Who navigate their black rooms so well
Dashing for the phone they never stumble.
Then I'll probably forget you as you leave
The cemetery, all of you grieving

As birch leaves circle wildly at your feet,
And a squirrel chitters in the nape of an oak,
And two jays quarrel, woodsmoke stings,
And I'm wishing whatever the dead wish.

December 9, 1993

Morning sunlight coats the hospital window,
A medicinal yellow, but without
Power to heal. Until today,
The dying woman's son and daughters
Pestered nurses, ambushed specialists,
Stopped anyone in surgical-green scrubs.

But now each time her respirator gulps
No one rushes out. Someone coughs
Across the hall, but she won't cough.
You have to breathe in order to do that.
On her left, the morphine drip. Above,

Her vital signs pulse like the stars
Over a field the son remembers
Now is not the moment to remember;
Nor the girl he wanted so to touch
He couldn't touch her; nor the dark rim
Of jersey pine around them.

What kind of hunger chooses *now*
To wonder if the girl still thinks of him?

Red digits, indicating oxygen, decrease.
The monitor's sequence of crests and clefts
Stiffens to a line. In short, she dies.
A nurse comes in to close her eyes, but can't.
Her daughters, crying, hold her swollen hands,

And her son—the one she nicknamed *Sta,*
The one whose ghoul-faces ruined snapshots,
The one she called her favorite until
He grew his hair and spoiled it—
This one, her youngest, massages her foot.

Villanelle After a Burial

Whatever they turned into wasn't ash.
Afraid of finding teeth, or something bony,
We had to face the aftermath of flesh.

Father's looked like coral: coarse, whitish,
Mother's looked like sand, but a fine dark gray.
Whatever they turned into wasn't ash—

More like a grainy noise that rose, a shush
We buried under their willow, spilled really.
We had to face it: the aftermath of flesh

Takes just two shovelfuls of dirt to finish
Off completely. Don't expect epiphanies,
Whatever they turned into. Wasn't *ash*

A dusty enough word, though, for the wish
That bits of spirit settle in what we see
After we face the aftermath of flesh?

We drove off in three pairs, each astonished
By awkward living talk, jittery keys.
We had to face the aftermath of flesh,
Whatever they turned into, wasn't ash.

The Work

You can go now, out of your life's
Compromise with life. You're ready to walk
Beneath the sycamores lined along the street
Like crowds welcoming their own liberation.

Yours will be a simple victory—one day
You'll choose to look out instead of down.
So leave and keep leaving; release
What holds you back, throw it aside

As someone who's not thirsty anymore
Flings a fan of water from a paper cup,
The water, for a second, taking flight,
Riveted with sunlight, air, and sound.

For you, no wings—just the habitual
Grip of hands. But notice how the dead
Skin begins to moult and fall away,
So even they grasp new things as new.

This victory will hurt and even kill you
Sometimes. A few welts won't heal. Remember,
As a child, how you stacked your wooden blocks,
And in a fit of serious pleasure kicked them down?—

It's bruising work you once mistook for play.

The Leap

Mandelstam at Cherdyn

Five nights without sleeping
And at their journey's end
A large white ward. Two beds
At right angles to the wall
Creak like doors opening
Whenever they shift in their sleep,
If they sleep. Exile's light
Is blindingly bright; who knows
If they'll get used to it?

Five nights without sleeping
And the voice he's heard all week
Won't cease. The voice
Of a poem? Of the state?
He can't say. All he knows
Is an exiled life's a conspiracy,
The future's an axe handle.

Five nights without sleeping
And she sinks into a watchful doze
Like sleeping & not sleeping.
He listens & studies the room,
Cross-legged on his bed,
Silent as paper. Even in sleep
She watches him listening.

Five nights without sleeping
And he's crouching on the sill
And she, behind him, can't stop
His body from lowering.
She grips the shoulders
Of his jacket—wrinkled, flapping—
Out of which his torso slips,
Then the dull thud & her cry.
She hangs the jacket on a nail

Five years later, in Moscow,
His arm so badly set he can't
Raise it over his head: the jacket
He forgets to take with him,
When the Cheka lead him away
For good; the jacket she's left
To hold at the door. *A leap,*
She'll remember, then memorize—
A leap & my mind is made whole.

Landlocked

In a basement crawl-space, a huddle of dreamed
Enemies, the bloodwork of sleep, you're still the one
Who played indoors, near the encyclopedia.
Prisoners compel you. In the morning
Your body dozes so quietly it's stranded
In a doorway with no door, on a canvas
Raft swept out to sea. From its wake

You watch your spirit drift closer.
One night it was an owl. Now it's so close
You feel it branch inside you, skeletal,
Like a hedge of sweating red berries, lethal
To anyone but you. Or when shallows wash in
Around a sandbar, you remember a tide
Lifting a moored ship. But now

You're flying over some midwestern state
You lived in or came from once, its patchwork
Of soyfields your future and past, its pockmarks
Of barns and housetops oases where facts
Hold the significance of dreams. You lie back
More deeply inland than you've ever been,
Relieved you've left no one essential behind.

On Fire

Element that sears and cleans:
Capricious, luscious . . .
Scarves of sweet, illegal smoke
Straying from a roadside blaze,
Cut limbs bubbling sap.

Sing a song of the blue advance,
A tide across old headlines, then
The kindling catches, then the logs,
Chimney stones suck up the process . . .
Gods, we burn what we inspire—

A child's curbside autumn spell
Intoned above those smoldering pyres:
Where there's smoke, there's hope,
Which flares again, again—elegant,
Seminal—as when a boy

Who spills a ring of gasoline
Across fresh-fallen snow, imagines
Cross hairs in his sights,
Then lights the edge
And flips the match out on his tongue.

About the Author

Born in Orange, New Jersey, in 1953, Steven Cramer received his B.A. in literature from Antioch College and his M.F.A. from the University of Iowa. He is the author of two previous collections of poetry, *The Eye That Desires to Look Upward* (The Galileo Press, 1987) and *The World Book* (Copper Beech Press, 1992). His poetry and criticism have appeared *The Atlantic Monthly*, *Harvard Review*, *The Nation*, *The New Republic*, *The Paris Review*, *Poetry*, *Triquarterly*, and numerous other periodicals. He has held editorial positions at David R. Godine, Publisher and at *The Atlantic Monthly*, and has taught writing at Boston University, M.I.T., and Tufts University. He currently teaches literature and poetry writing at Bennington College. His awards include grants from the Artists Foundation of Massachusetts, the National Endowment for the Arts, and the Alan Collins fellowship to the Bread Loaf Writer's Conference. With his wife, Hilary Rao, and their daughter Charlotte, he divides his time between Vermont and Massachusetts.